EASTER COLORING AND ACTIVITY BOOK FOR KIDS

This Coloring book belongs to:

____

ISBN-13: 978-1983967818

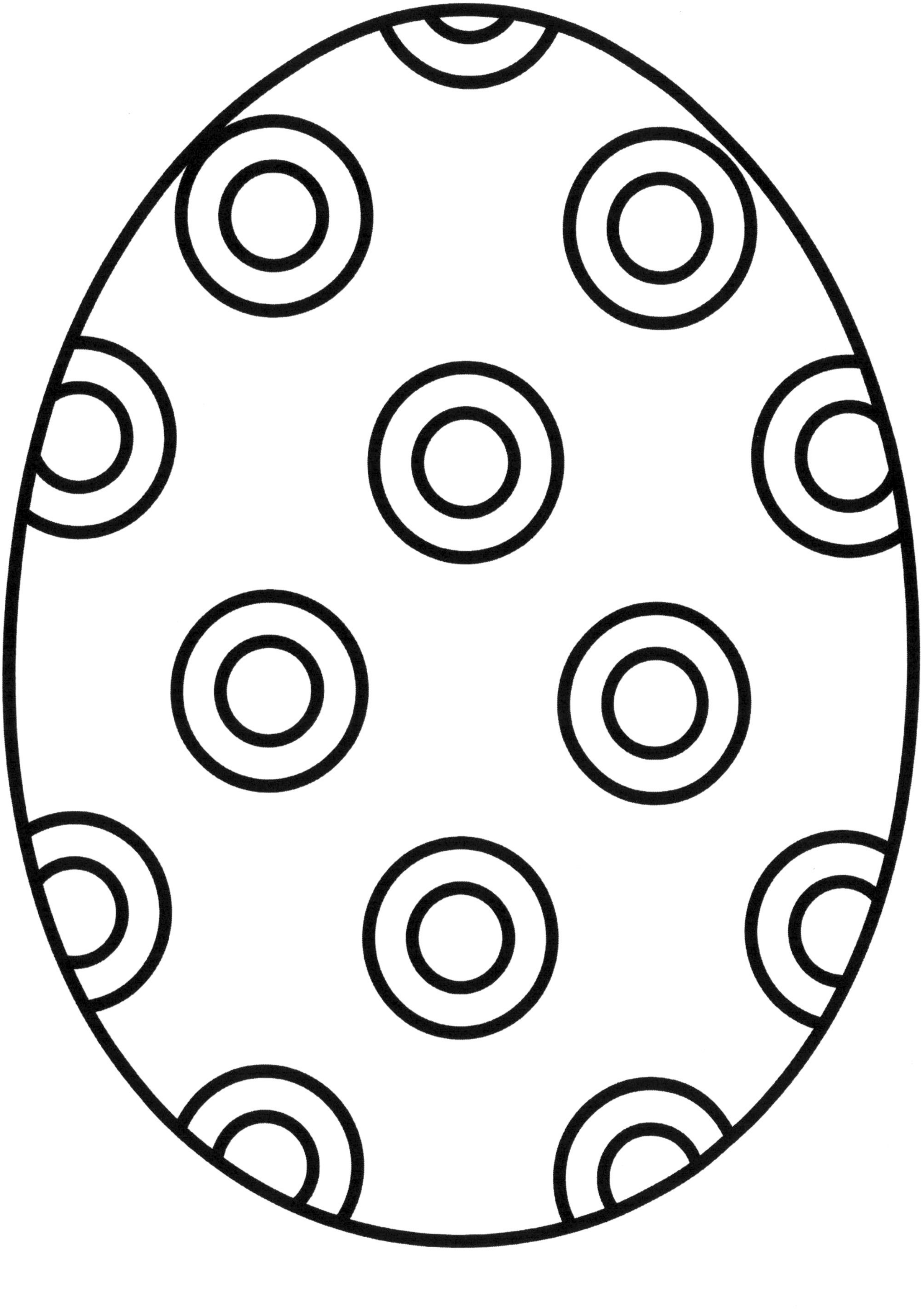

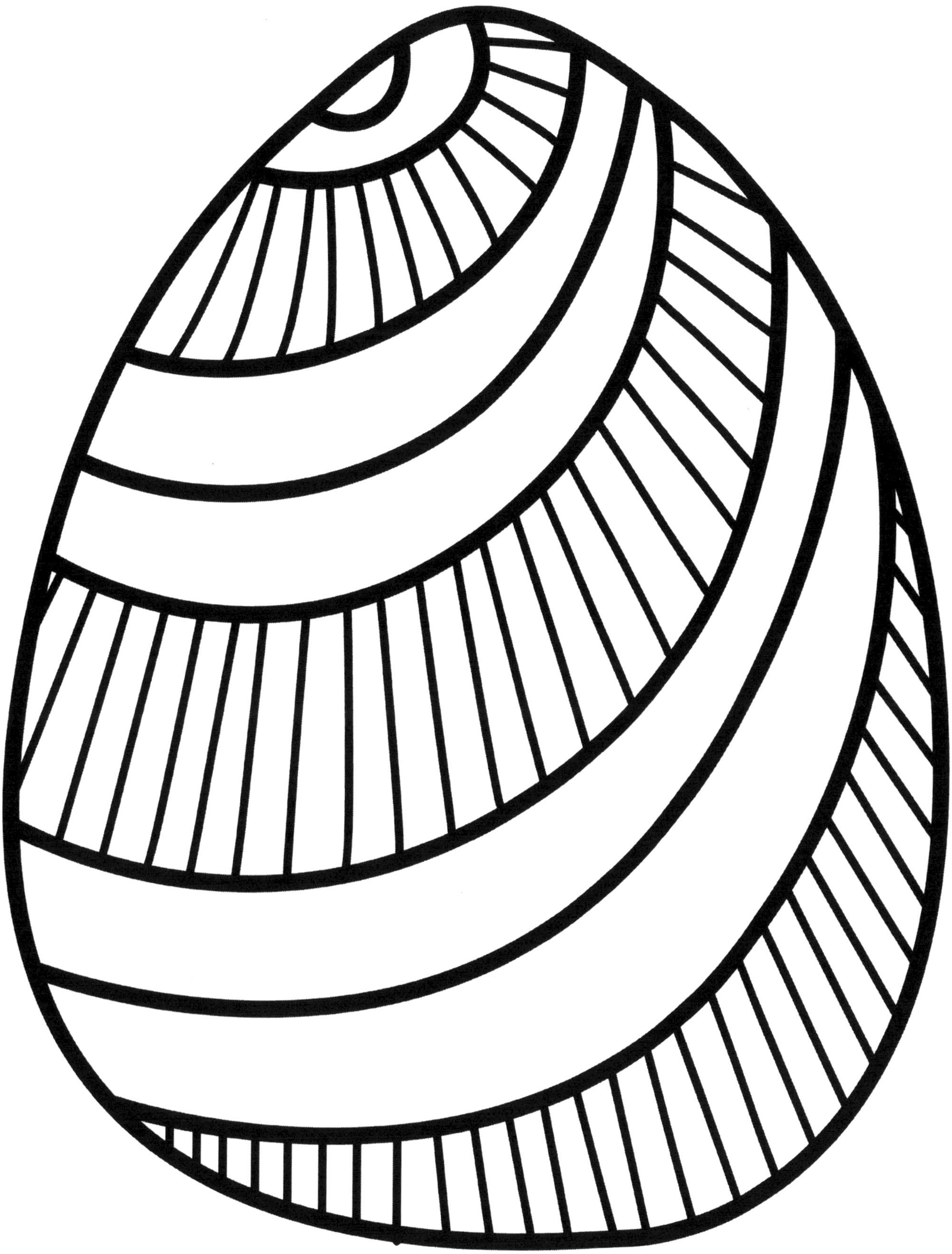

Complete the following
dot to dot activities

Activity - 1

Draw a line from dot number 1 to dot number 2, then from dot number 2 to dot number 3, 3 to 4, and so on. Continue to join the dots until you have connected all the numbered dots. Then, color the picture!

Activity - 2

Draw a line from dot number 1 to dot number 2, then from dot number 2 to dot number 3, 3 to 4, and so on. Continue to join the dots until you have connected all the numbered dots. Then, color the picture!

Activity - 3

Draw a line from dot number 1 to dot number 2, then from dot number 2 to dot number 3, 3 to 4, and so on. Continue to join the dots until you have connected all the numbered dots. Then color the picture!

Answer to Activity - 1

Answer to Activity - 2

Answer to Activity - 3

Draw your own designs
on the following
3 blank Easter eggs

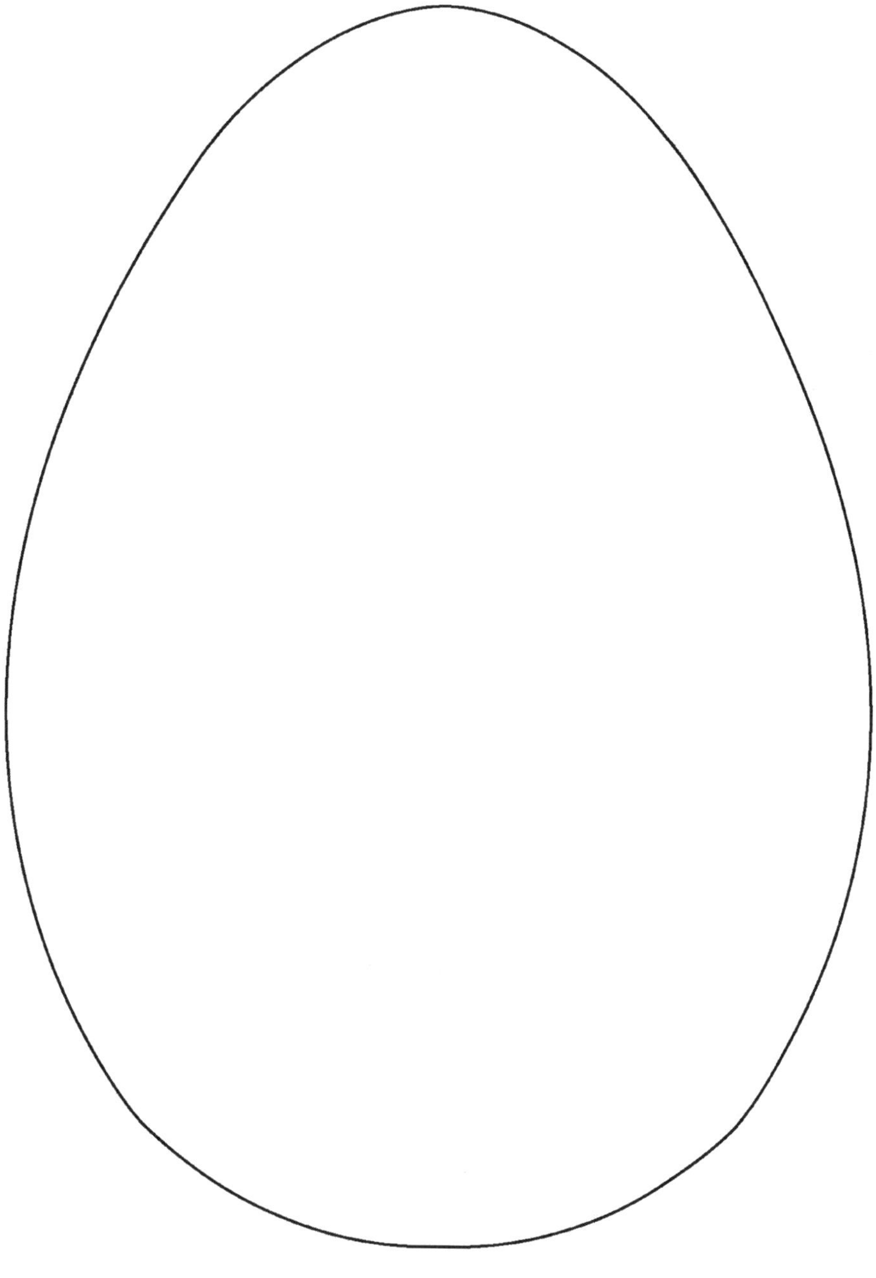

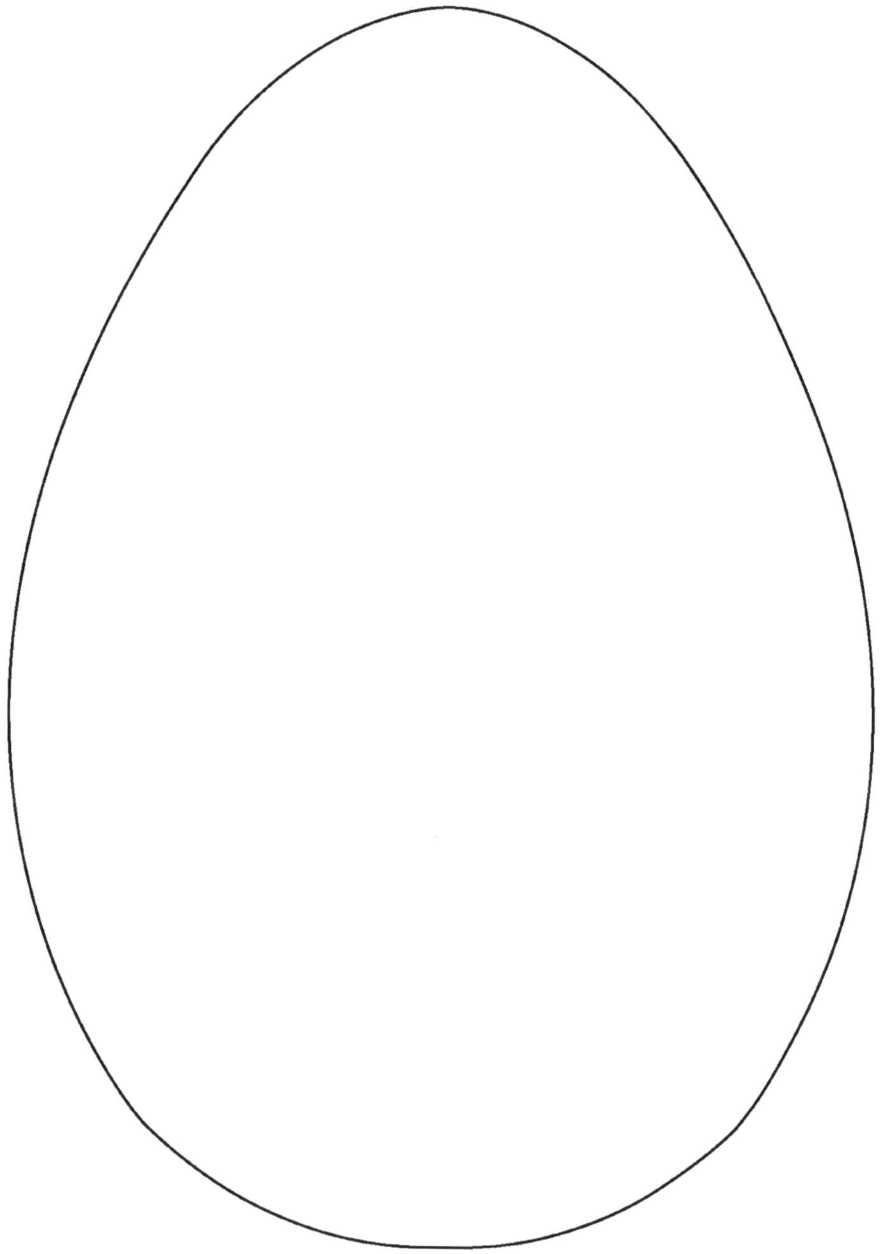

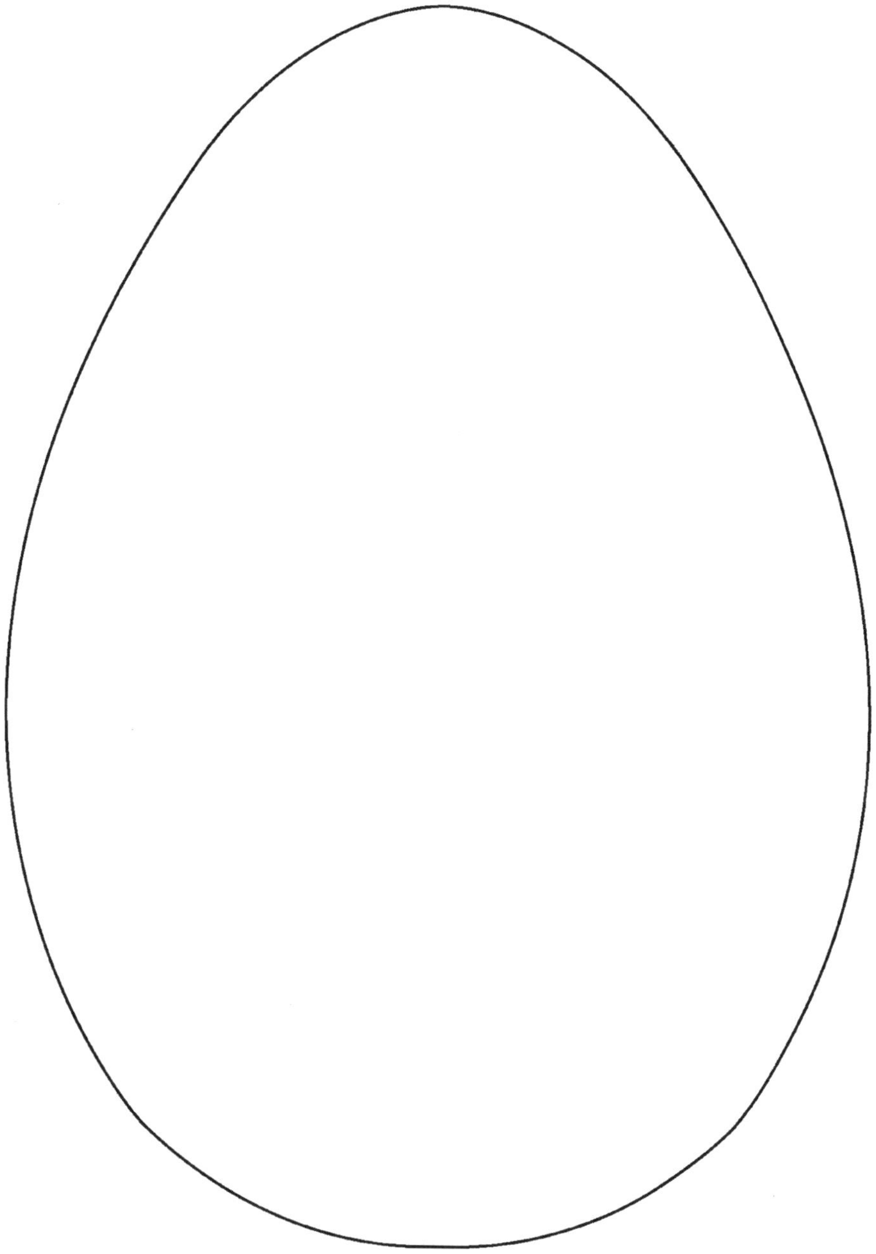

Bonus!

Two sets of each coloring page

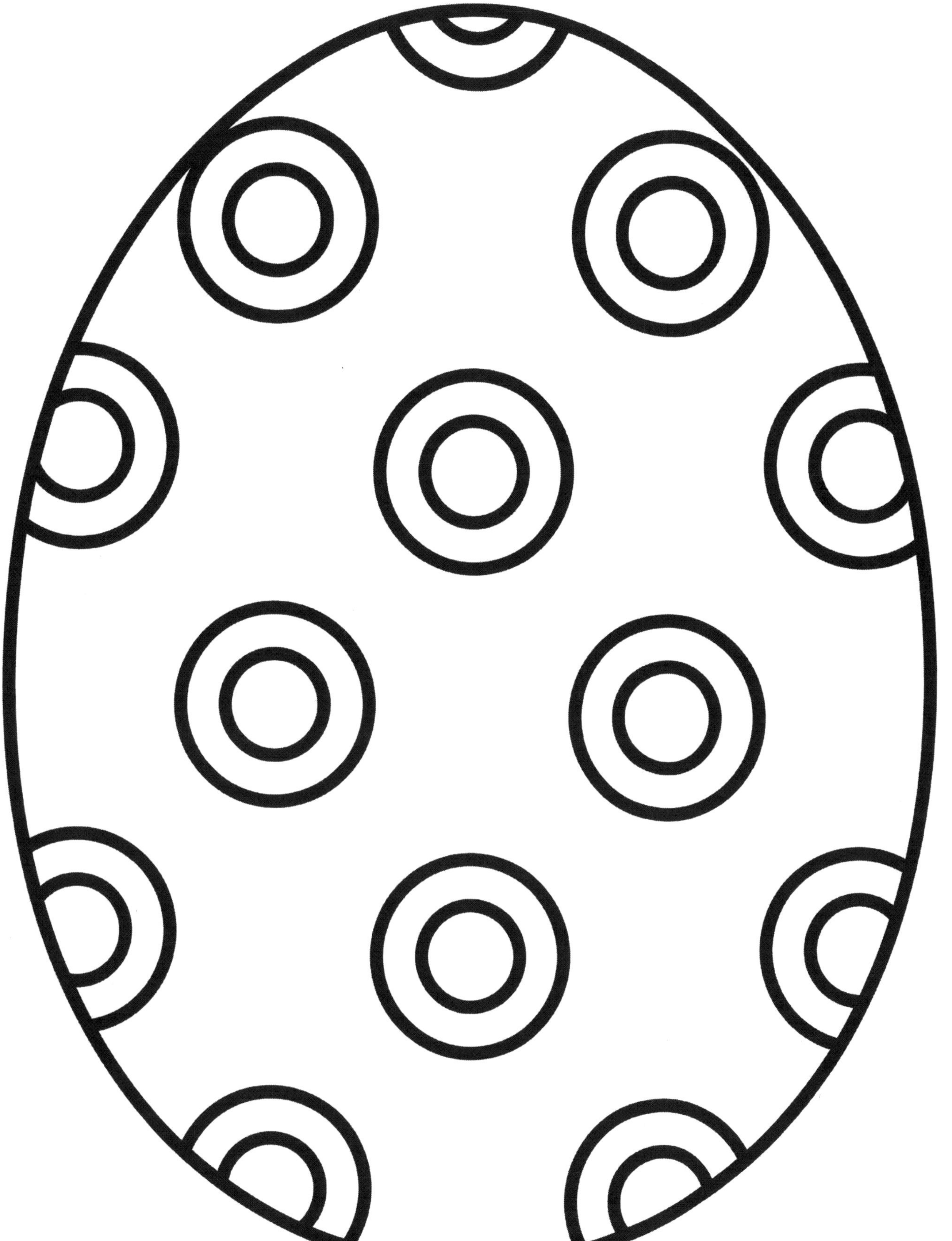

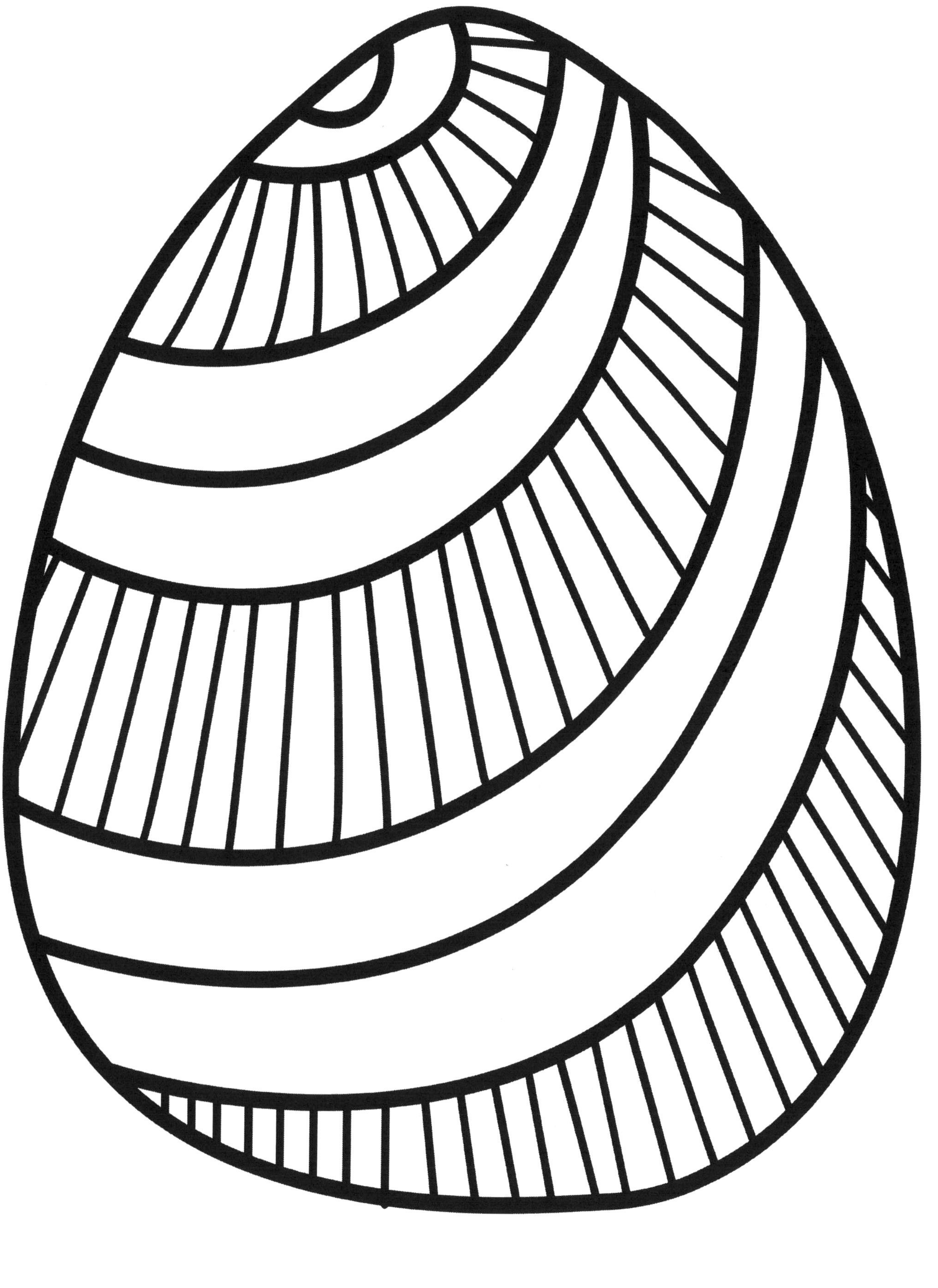

Activity - 1

Draw a line from dot number 1 to dot number 2, then from dot number 2 to dot number 3, 3 to 4, and so on. Continue to join the dots until you have connected all the numbered dots. Then, color the picture!

Activity - 2

Draw a line from dot number 1 to dot number 2, then from dot number 2 to dot number 3, 3 to 4, and so on. Continue to join the dots until you have connected all the numbered dots. Then, color the picture!

Activity - 3

Draw a line from dot number 1 to dot number 2, then from dot number 2 to dot number 3, 3 to 4, and so on. Continue to join the dots until you have connected all the numbered dots. Then color the picture!

67493705R00075

Made in the USA
Middletown, DE
22 March 2018